Books shoul'

Books should be returned on or before the
last date stamped below.

JUL 39 3 4

9 JUN 1987

9 FEB 1990        - 4 SEP 1990

2 9 JUN 1987

2 1 FEB 1990      2 OCT 1990
2 4 APR 1990      2 6 OCT 1990

2 0 JUL 1987

2 7 AUG 1987                        2 3 NOV 1990

2 7 OCT 1987    2 MAY 1990

2 7 APR 1988                        2 6 JAN 1991

                3 1 MAY 1990       - 8 JUL 1991

1 3 JUL 1988
1 6 NOV 1989    2 8 JUN 1990       1 2 AUG 1991
19 Dec 89
                                    3 0 MAR 1992

2 8 DEC 1989    2 5 JUL 1990       2 0 1 3 APR 1992
                                    2 0 NOV 1992

D0267692

# SAND and SILENCE

*—Lost Villages of the North—*

**D.P. Willis, MA, MLitt, FSA Scot.**

ISBN 0 906 265 07 X

Published by the Centre for Scottish Studies, University of Aberdeen, 1986

# FOREWORD

Douglas Willis is the Principal teacher of Geography at Fortrose Academy in the Black Isle. He has become a familiar figure on the Extra-Mural circuit in the North of Scotland where his twinned skills of geographer and ornithologist have produced many fascinating talks. This booklet has arisen out of these interests. The author has drawn together the strands of evidence which help us to understand the life and death of these villages. Paradoxically the sand grains which led to their demise as settlements were to lead in more than one case to the survival of their physical remains. Once again I am grateful to Mr Jim Livingston of the Department of Geography for his field photography including the cover.

J S Smith

## INTRODUCTION

*Ill fares the land to hastening ills a prey*
Oliver Goldsmith<br>The Deserted Village

It is in the nature of human settlements that some have flourished and grown while others have known stagnation and decline. The complete loss of a community of folk from the face of the land is, however, a happening of particular interest. Such "lost villages" undoubtedly have a special appeal to the imagination, allowing great scope in conjuring up pictures of a vanished past.

In my mind I retain a vivid recollection of a visit to a deserted village site in the green pastoral lowlands of England, where outlines of curving plough ridges and ground markings brought powerfully to mind the life and times of one of those lost villages of the south poetically eulogised by Goldsmith and so well described by Maurice Beresford and W G Hoskins. In the half light of a late summer evening, it was a powerful experience to stand among those last reminders of a vanished village, as the murmur of a turtle dove carried across the stillness, and the lengthening shadows fell across the land once intimately known to generations of farming folk, but now deserted and silent.

Such inland lost settlements are poignant reminders of human tragedy and changing fortune, but in a coastal setting there are reminders, too, of human situations in which the people who lived there were the victims of an environmental change beyond their control. At several places around our sandy coasts there is evidence of the power of wind and sand to swamp and bury human settlement, but nowhere else is there a grouping of sites like the northern one described in the pages that follow.

These lost "villages" of the north are, in reality, a very mixed group of settlement types. Over the years each of them has had a special appeal for me, for each tells its own tale of a lost human presence and offers its own present day interest. This brief survey of the four sites is an attempt to reflect this, and at the same time to try to share their appeal more widely, hopefully providing a useful introduction for those who would seek out these fascinating places for themselves. In no way is this an attempt to shed new light on old mysteries, but rather to pull together a few threads from the fabric of our northern past.

Beresford, M (1954) *The Lost Villages of England.*
Hoskins, W G (1955) *The Making of the English Landscape.*

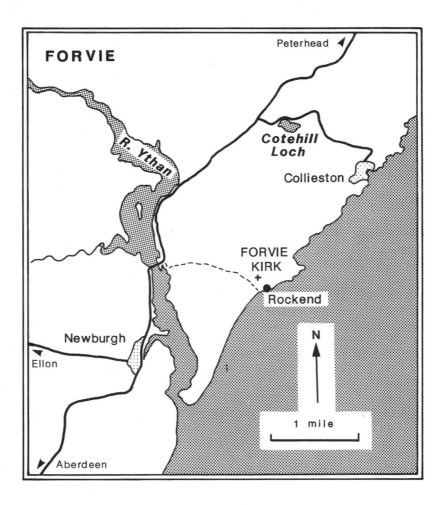

## FORVIE

*The wondrous weird and waste tract known as the Sands of Forvie*
William Ferguson of Kinmundy, 1888[1]

On the knuckle of North-east Scotland, just a little to the north of Aberdeen, the small river Ythan flows quietly into the grey North Sea. From its inland infancy to its slow, mature meandering among the fertile farmlands of lowland Aberdeenshire the river has collected the rich dark silt that forms its centuries-old estuarine mudflats. In the brackish mingling of emptying river and flooding sea, mussel beds line tidal banks where eider ducks gather in a life-consuming search for food. Close by the river which gave it its locational suffix nestles the village of Newburgh-on-Ythan, once the new burgh and outport for the upstream bridging point of Ellon, and now a convenient commuter settlement for the oil-rich 'Granite City' to the south. But across the Ythan's fertile ooze, where lines of piping oystercatchers follow the ebb tide, and beyond the bustle of the village, there lies a wholly different world; a world of sand and silence and ancient lost settlement.

Hemmed in by the river on one side and the open sea on the other, the peninsula of Forvie is an inviting place on a warm summer's day when sandwich terns scream above the dunes at the river mouth and grouse cocks boldly proclaim their territories from heathery tussocks. But when the force of an easterly gale rips at the very roots of the anchoring bent grass and whistles round the stonework of the salmon fishers' Rockend bothy, Forvie becomes a place transformed. At these wild times, when white sea spume flies in across the moor, it is hard to think that such a forbidding place could ever have been home to a community of people. The lonely, gnarled old trees that cringe away from the salt-laden winds tell their own tale of wild winters past and of the rigours of existence in such an exposed land. Yet, to the seeing eye, Forvie's landscape still bears the marks of the folk who, down through the centuries, knew the moor in all its varying moods.

\* \* \*

The story of the earliest human interest is written not in stone foundations, however, but in undistinguished midden heaps of shells that line the Ythan's estuarine shore. From these remains we may conjure up a shadowy picture of an ancient race travelling the searoad of the north, and making landfall wherever conditions seemed most favourable.

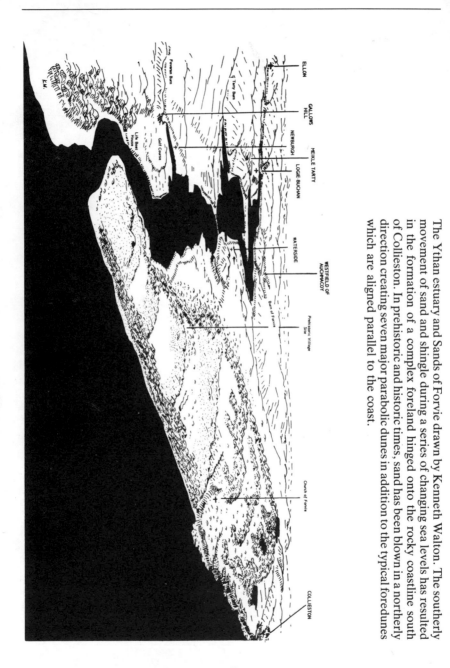

The Ythan estuary and Sands of Forvie drawn by Kenneth Walton. The southerly movement of sand and shingle during a series of changing sea levels has resulted in the formation of a complex foreland hinged onto the rocky coastline south of Collieston. In prehistoric and historic times, sand has been blown in a northerly direction creating seven major parabolic dunes in addition to the typical foredunes which are aligned parallel to the coast.

The sheltered river mouth of the Ythan was, doubtless, such a place.

T F Jamieson, 19th Century pioneer in geomorphology in the North-east, was the first to remark upon these ancient waterside remains with their associated flints, and noted: "On turning up the ground with a spade I found a stratum of black carbonaceous matter below which the reddish clay subsoil was quite discoloured as if there had been numerous fires".[2]

His conclusions from the varied finds on the site were that "Along both sides of the Ythan, near its junction with the sea, there seems to have existed a settlement of people who used flint tools, and lived a good deal upon the shellfish that are found in the adjoining estuary".

Such unpretentious midden heaps serve now as sole reminders of those distant folk and the monotony of their diet, but it should be borne in mind that there has been a long continuity of interest in the shellfish resources of the estuary, both as a basic food source and as bait for fishing the coastal waters. Forvie's shell middens must, therefore, be treated with some caution, for they may serve both to confirm and confuse the early history of man in the place. However, the fact that such remains were interbedded with layers of blown sand is itself a commentary on the uncertain and changing nature of this coastal environment, and a pointer to the difficulty that man has had to contend with through time.

* * *

Apart from the evidence of these early finds last century, it had long been guessed that the interior of Forvie Moor might once also have been the site of more extensive prehistoric settlement. Sharp-eyed visitors frequently chanced upon flint flakes and even arrow heads among the sand. The presence of such a valuable resource in these northern parts may possibly seem unusual, but while flint is more commonly associated with more southerly places, early North-east man did have access to a local supply of the material in a low ridge running across the flat plain of Buchan. Apart from such chance finds, however, the numerous antiquarian naturalists of last century found little else to augment their meagre knowledge of the ancient history of Forvie, and, indeed, many decades were to pass before the moor was ready to reveal any other facet of its past.

During 1951 and 1952, a substantial movement of sand uncovered an unexpected assemblage of nineteen late Bronze Age- Early Iron Age hut circles. These were the material remains of a prehistoric village community, in fact, the existence of which had hitherto been unknown to those who had tried to probe the secrets of the place. Such a find was clearly of considerable local interest, and a team from the University of Aberdeen, guided by Dr Douglas Simpson, doyen of North-east antiquarians, began an examination of the site. From this investigation William Kirk of the Geography Department was able to reconstruct a picture of "a small community cultivating the light sandy soils near their circular homesteads, grinding their own grain in stone querns, pasturing sheep, pigs, and oxen, adding to their diet by hunting deer in the interior and fishing in the estuary, and possessing a dry site within easy reach of water and a copious supply of raw materials such as flint".[3]

Such a clear picture of its prehistoric past had been denied the countless earlier visitors who had traversed the moor in search of clues to its life and landscape of ancient times. Their preoccupation had, understandably, been with the faint outline of the well known mediaeval kirk set deep within the heart of the moor, and with the colourful local accounts of its nearby lost village. Interest in the old ruin was considerable, but little was known of its true history. The parish minister, writing in the New Statistical Account, observed that "The foundation of the Old Kirk of Forvie is still visible, being the only vestige throughout the whole sands, commonly called the links, which indicates that this district was once the habitation of man. Graves have been discovered round it, but nothing found in them except a few bones".[4] Indeed, to the 19th Century naturalists, even locating the site was not always easy, it seems, as William Ferguson's account relates:

"We crossed ..... in search of the ruins of the Old Kirk, but though we had found it on former visits, this time we failed to do so, it is so wonderfully hidden among the sandhills near the shore. It is a wild and lonely scene - no human being visible except perhaps along one beaten pathway on the horizon a long train of fishermen and fisherwomen, returning from a six mile tramp to Ythan estuary, laden with mussels and lobworms for bait. But this track lies along the western verge of the sands and when you leave it, even for a few yards, you are in the heart of a wide solitude, the haunt of great coveys of grouse and innumerable rabbits".[5]

\* \* \*

Away from the riverside, when the summer bloom of bell heather lightens the dark face of the moor, and breeding terns raucously assert their presence among the sand dunes, it is hard to think of days when folk once called the interior of this place their home. But it should always be borne in mind that the present pattern of our rural landscape was not one familiar to the farming folk of the past. Today's frontier of cultivation in these productive agricultural lowlands has pushed hard against the moor. Yet the improvers' ploughs were never to tame this last relic of wild lowland heath, for the tide of farming improvement was not to engulf the sandy lands of Forvie, with their lasting imprint of more ancient farming patterns.

To understand the apparent paradox of why an area which once attracted farmers should later come to repel them, it is necessary at once to appreciate the needs of early man and the forces that may be at work through time on such an uncertain coastal environment. To begin with, the technology of early North-east man was ill-fitted for dealing with lands which today might seem the most favourable to work. Primitive implements were better suited to tilling light, treeless, and sometimes calcareous coastal areas than the heavy, wet "clarty clay" of the landward interior. Today, one of the joys of a visit to Forvie is contact with its abundant wildlife, and there is no reason to suggest that things were not always so. In the past such natural resources were there for the harvesting, whether in the form of nesting birds and their eggs or the small dark summer fruits of crowberry. And there has, doubtless, also been a long continuity of interest in fishing, for the site of the village lies some one and a half miles south of the old fishing settlement of Collieston, and a short distance from the Rockend salmon fishing bothy. It seems, therefore, to have been well positioned for a dual economy, based both on land and sea. Sitting as it does almost hidden beside a small burn deeply downcut into the sand and underlying red glacial till, the ruined kirk is today a scant memorial to the life and times of the folk who worked the rigs around it, and worshipped within its hallowed walls. It was inevitable that such a lonely and poignant reminder of a long lost mediaeval village should have intrigued the generations of visitors who experienced Forvie's "weird feeling of profound solitude" so evocatively described by William Ferguson at the end of last century. Even today, to judge by the steady trek of summer visitors across the moorland path the place has lost none of its power to draw the visitors to seek out its mute remains.

\* \* \*

But what had caused the demise of Forvie's village? Looking across the humps and hollows of the peninsula today, it is not hard to deduce that some shift in the pattern of distribution of the sand must have taken the life from that community of folk, but when and why are questions that are difficult to answer. Local legend asserted that the 18th of August, 1413, was a day to remember along the North-east coast, a day when a fierce easterly gale blocked the mouth of the River Don with sand. A little further along the coast, Forvie was said to have succumbed to the moving mass of sand in that one, fateful blow.

But it would have been strange, indeed, if local folklore had not held out its own solutions to the mystery. A 16th Century 'preacher of the gospel' is reputed to have asserted that "the folks of Forvie suffered this heavy judgement because they were Papists and grossly ignorant".[6]

And folklore has also handed down another, altogether more romantic interpretation of that fateful act of overblowing by sand. This also embodies the notion that such a catastrophic event must surely be the working of some fateful scheme of retribution. Tradition relates that the orphaned heiress (some versions have it that there were three) was duped by a scheming uncle. In order to secure her inheritance for his own wicked ends the villain of the piece cast the hapless maiden adrift in a boat. As it drifted away from the land, there carried towards the shore a plaintive sound, now embodied in the local traditional folklore stanza:

"If ever madenis Malyson
Ded licht upon drie lande
Let nocht be funde on Forvy's glebes
But thistle bente and sande".

Inevitably this curse, colourful though it is, must be regarded as a dubious reason for the overwhelming of the village. In local folklore it probably belongs to that same category of what might be termed "retrospective prophesying", well known, for example, further north in the Black Isle where "prophesies" seem to have been invented to fit certain later occurrences and then attributed to the famous Brahan Seer.

\* \* \*

In an attempt to shed some more light on the uncertain story of Forvie's past a local doctor set to work to excavate the ruined kirk at the end of last century. From no great distance beneath the surface sand was brought to the light of day once more a "piscina" - a roughly shaped stone basin used by the celebrant of the holy sacrament. But after this promising find Forvie was reluctant to yield much more of the true secret of its past. As a result, only a little is known of the history of this kirk among the sand anciently dedicated to St Adamnan. In the 16th Century, however, there is an interesting record of the church of "Furvie" having been given by King James VI to King's College in Aberdeen.[7]

The ensuing centuries have not dealt kindly with the place, and it seems likely that the salmon fishers removed some of the building stone to construct their bothy at nearby Rockend. Today, the low walls are turf-topped and encrusted with lichens that richly pattern the dark stones in shades of grey and yellow. In the absence of more definite fact concerning the village's fate we can only now let the mind conjure up its own images of the past. From inside the old walls, as the sea air gusts among the stone work, we may speculate on the thoughts of the folk who gathered in that place of worship in the face of an impending environmental catastrophe they were powerless to prevent. In the distance must have loomed ominously large the towering mounds of sand that were soon to advance and draw a curtain of silence over the entire place. But the ruined kirk is not their sole surviving memorial. Here and there the seeing eye may vaguely discern a ground surface faintly etched in patterns of ancient plough rigs, the very life blood of the agricultural community that was fated to perish beneath the suffocating sand. Whatever the exact circumstances of the disaster, it is clear that these last worshippers in Forvie's kirk were doomed to see their precious lands taken from them, and their homes and kirk lost from sight beneath an engulfing march of sand which they were powerless to stop.

\* \* \*

But could it really have been like that? Did things happen in a sudden catastrophic way, or were the signs of impending disaster perhaps obvious long before? One of the greatest features of interest in Forvie for the geographer is what Kenneth Walton saw as the "interplay of physical processes and the changing fortunes of the inhabitants of the coastal area,"[8] and William Kirk as human history "being literally interwoven with a story of environmental change".[9]

In fact, current knowledge of the mechanics of mass sand movement and of the variables involved in it would suggest that the truth is more likely to lie in some gradual process of sand movement which had been threatening the lands of Forvie over a much longer period of time. Inevitably, the strongest storms would have been capable of the most spectacular movement of loose material, but it is unthinkable that one gale, however fierce, or from whatever quarter, could have resulted in such a remarkably rapid change in the fortunes of the place. Once the chain of events involving sand movement was underway, however, things could only get worse, and the inexorable march of the loose material would certainly have threatened any farmlands that lay in its path. Even as late as the mid 18th Century, there had been such a considerable northward blowing of sand that the Earl or Errol, proprietor of the estate, found it necessary to reduce his tenant's rent. The relevant rent roll, for example, notes that "Alexander Thoirs, tenant in Whiteness,

Mains of Collieston, and Cothill, and of Kirkton of Slains, has got since the commencement of his tack, and is entitled during the currency of the same, £23 6s 8f Scots money of abatement of account of damage done to the possession by sanding".[10] By the 19th Century, however, it would appear that the massive shifts of sand had virtually ceased, and the present day pattern had largely been established. The writer of the New Statistical parish account, for example, noted that "On the north-west boundary there is an immense ridge of sand which is still encroaching on the land, but so slowly that if a judgement may be formed of the progress over the past 12 years, ages must have elapsed ere such a large district of the country could have been overwhelmed".[11]

In recent times the degree of change has been fairly small, although minor movements along the seaward edge appear to have been something of an inconvenience to the smugglers who once plied their trade along Forvie's coast. At the end of last century, for example, there was a strong local tradition of quantities of gin having been hidden among the bents and so covered by shifting sand that they were entirely lost, and remain buried there to this day. Indeed, we can thank the Forvie smugglers for confirmation of the greatly reduced pattern of sand move-ment last century, for it is recorded that one "David Watson, the last of the east coast smugglers who died in the year 1870, at the advanced age of 96, said that during his life-time he had never known of the drifts of sand making any serious inroads into cultivation".[12]

\* \* \*

From our perspective in time, therefore, it is clear that Forvie's fate in the historical record has been intimately linked with the movements of the sand in which the peninsula is covered. The existence of such vast accumulations of fine sand to accomplish this task should occasion no real surprise when it is remembered that uncontrolled torrents of glacial meltwater once carried an enormous load of ground-down rock to the sea. When subjected to the force of strong winds coming in off the sea, these fine beach deposits, consisting mostly of hard quartz grains, can easily blow inland and in time advance like a dry wave. Thus the history of Forvie landscape is interpreted by geographers in terms of seven dune waves arranged at right angles to the coast. The youngest lies at the peninsula's southernmost tip, with the landscape becoming progressively older to the north, culminating in the first or oldest ridge that delimits the moor's northern flank. It is, therefore, against the background of this dune wave system and its development that the story of Forvie's human occupation has been enacted.

* * *

Now, however, Forvie's heather-clad moor retains only a few last reminders of its vanished past, and the area has survived as an island of unreclaimed moorland that serves to highlight the scale of man's transformation of the lowland landscape of the North-east. But changing human perception of the value of such an undisturbed area has given Forvie Moor an added value and a new role. Because of its great significance as a sand dune system and as unreclaimed coastal heathland, with all the associated ecological richness, the area was designated the Sands of Forvie National Nature Reserve in 1959. Indeed, it was one of the first such reserves, and two decades later its area was augmented by the addition of the Ythan estuary, a rare example these days of a largely unspoiled and unpolluted estuarine area, making the total reserve one of the finest protected ecological sites in the northern landscape. The river mouth dunes support the largest breeding colony of sandwich terns in Scotland, and the moorland nesting eider ducks form the greatest breeding concentration of this species along the whole of the British coast. One of the finest wildlife sights of the moor is that of well-camouflaged eider mothers and their following lines of fluffy ducklings negotiating the rank heather on the early summer trek to the shore. By contrast, on the cliff section where the moor falls abruptly away to the sea, fulmar petrels cackle hysterically from their bare nesting ledges. Their numbers have greatly increased, but the "great coveys" of red grouse encountered by the 19th Century seekers after the lost village seem to have all but disappeared.

As Forvie's summer days fade slowly into autumn, seasonal mists coupled with unfavourable patterns of wind sometimes interrupt the southward migration of small birds from north European breeding grounds, and mornings often find tired and disorientated small birds as rare as bluethroats and black redstarts skulking about among the scattered low bushes. Even the cold silent days bring their own rewards with the occasional sight of roe deer foraging for food among snow-filled dune hollows. At such a time, and in such a setting, there is a rare and desolate beauty about the face of the winter moor, though few human visitors are around to appreciate it.

It is not only the birds and mammals, however, that add to the interest of Forvie for the visitor prepared to walk across the moorland path. On moist ground above the sea cliffs, pale green butterworts lie like strangely coloured starfish, their ever open fleshy leaves offering a sticky and fatal welcome to any passing insect. And it is in these damp hollows also that the lovely Grass of Parnassus has its late summer blooming of delicately veined white flowers above long stems, surely one of the loveliest of all our native plants.

In addition to these present day attractions, however, Forvie's fascination for the visitor lies deeply rooted in its past. When the silence of evening falls round the ruins of its ancient kirk the summer cries of nesting seabirds carry on the updraught from the shore and become lost in the loneliness of a place that once resounded to the sounds of a village now silenced by sand. At such times, against the timeless background dirge of the sea, it is easy to feel that Forvie's past and present are somehow mingled as one. And however much we may dismiss the old local tradition of the maiden's malison as superstitious myth, we cannot but acknowledge that in today's covering of thistle, bent and sand nature has achieved her own fulfilment of an ancient prophesy.

1. Ferguson W (1888) The Sands of Forvie *Trans Buchan Field Club* Vol 1 pp 22ff

2. Jamieson T F (1865) On Some Remains of the Stone Period in the Buchan District of Aberdeenshire *Proceedings of the Society of Antiquaries of Scotland* Vol VI pp 240ff

3. Kirk W (1953) Prehistoric Sites at the Sands of Forvie, Aberdeenshire *Aberdeen University Review* Vol XXXV pp 150-171

4. *New Statistical Account* (1845)

5. Ferguson W (1901) The Sands of Forvie in *The Book of Ellon* pp 104-110

6. Ferguson W Ibid

7. Pratt J B (1870) *Buchan* p29

8. Walton K (1966) The Ythan Estuary, Aberdeenshire in *Geography as Human Ecology* p30

9. Kirk W Ibid

10. Dalgarno J (1896) *From the Brig o' Balgownie to the Bullers o' Buchan* p13

11. New Statistical Account (1845)

12. Dalgarno J p14

## RATTRAY

*Keep Mormond Hill a handspike high*
*And Rattray Briggs ye'll ne'er come nigh*

Old Mariner's Warning

The old seafarer's warning about the dangers of shipwreck on the treacherous rocks of Rattray Head was once a very necessary one for those who ventured along that notorious stretch of coast. Today, the blinking light of Rattray Head lighthouse sitting atop its convict-built plinth has removed the necessity of scanning the landward horizon for the outline of Mormond Hill. This wind-blasted corner of Buchan seems now a lonely place, largely deserted of human settlement. The coastguards have long gone, leaving behind a forlorn and empty row of cottages, while automation of the light has removed the lighthouse families who once lived a real end-of-the-road existence in this outermost edge of the North-east corner.

But things were clearly not always so, and what seems now a forbidding place was once the site of a lost village which for a while even aspired to royal burgh status. The Castlehill of Rattray, which lies on the eastern side of the site of the lost village and certainly predated it, would seem to have an overly pretentious name for such a humble grassy mound. Yet it belonged once to a pattern of early castle sites stretching along the North-east coast. Their presence, clearly related to coastal defence, has been associated with the Viking forays, but later the Comyn Earls, whose original homeland was far from Buchan in the lowland plain of Flanders, exerted their influence over this part of the world and possibly continued the protection of the land from seaborne attack. Indeed, there has been a long continuity of interest in the mound for strategic purposes, for although all traces of the original fortification have long since vanished, a World War II concrete pill-box now crowns its top. But if there is no evidence of the ancient castle of Rattray, there is certainly striking visual proof of a past human presence in the ruins of the nearby chapel of St Mary's. The stone-built chapel's origins are generally held to lie in the 13th Century, although a stone block erroneously gives a date of 911 AD. Of this spurious reminder of the chapel's age, John Milne, LLD, who took a great interest in the history of the area at the turn of the century wrote: "I should not regard it as a sacrilege if some person deposited the stone in the bottom of the loch".[1]

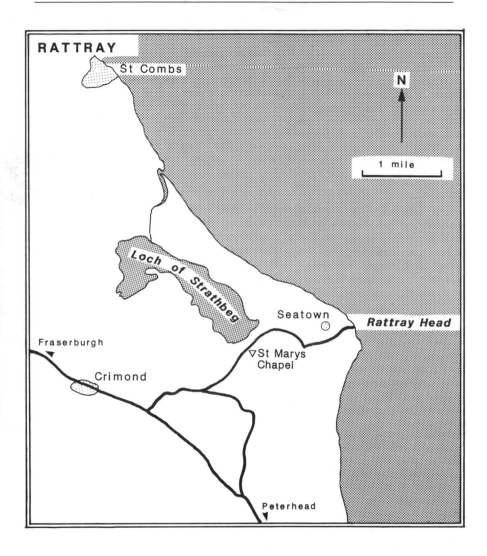

The chapel is first mentioned in connection with a gift made to it by William Comyn, Earl of Buchan, in the early 13th Century. History records that William Comyn granted in free alms for ever to the Chapel of the Blessed Virgin Mary, in the town of Rattray, an annual rent of two stones of wax, payable at Whitsunday from the lands and the mill of Strichen and Kindrought.[2] The beeswax would, of course, have been used for the supply of candles for use in services. In 1342 Sir Archibald Douglas received the Lordship of Rattray, and in his charter there was mention of a harbour. Milne describes the likely nature of the settlement of Rattray as it then was, "The townland had been a commonty where the townsfolk pastured their cows and dug sods and clay for house-building. Their houses were not of stone and lime at this time. A common way of building a house was to lay down a layer of sods, and so on, the corners being well rounded and the walls sloping inwards. The fire was in the middle of the floor well away from the combustible wall. The townspeople would have had enclosed gardens and small fields with corn with an enclosing feal dyke, outside of which the muir was common to all".[2]

Following the Reformation, Rattray was elevated to the status of royal burgh. The charter of erection, dated 1563, gave its burgesses the right to erect a market cross and hold their own weekly market, as well as two fairs per year. The hope that the settlement's new found importance would lead to its people building their homes in stone and lime does not, however, seem to have had any measure of fulfilment.

The folk whose home was that extremity of the cold shoulder of Buchan pursued a way of life that was based both on land and sea, and the harbour, anciently called Starnakeppie, provided a sheltered haven for their fishing boats. In Macfarlane's Geographical Collections, Alexander Hepburn mentions "the village of Rattray, famous for codfish, which the inhabitants take in great plenty, and have the best way of drying and curing them".[3] Even so, things were apparently not to work out very successfully for the settlement, for the 1696 Aberdeenshire Poll Book could list the presence of only seventeen adults.[4] However, it may be that some of the fermtouns round about had some connection with the sea through the harbour of Starnakeppie, for neighbouring Bilbo has two seamen and one fisher listed for it, while Broadlands of Rattray had two fishers resident there.

\* \* \*

Apart from the long-standing chapel walls, there is now no surviving trace of the royal burgh of Rattray. The exhortation to build in more permanent materials was clearly not heeded, and as a result the face of the land today recalls little of the deserted settlement. But place-names can sometimes help recall what material remains fail to record, and the field name "Shore Wynd" is evocative of the little lanes that lead seawards from the fishing villages of the North-east coast. As a boy, I recall also an old farmer in the area telling me that a white horse working the land once put its leg down a depression in the ground, and when it came back out it was covered in black soot. The animal, it seems, had stumbled into the remains of some ancient hearth.

Rattray's *raison d'etre* had clearly lain in its role as sheltered anchorage on an exposed and dangerous coastline. Any physical change that might threaten this vulnerable inlet would inevitably spell disaster and ruin for the folk whose living depended on its continued existence, and disaster it seemed was not too far away. Rattray's coastal embayment owed its shelter to the protecting shingle bar that had been building slowly southwards for centuries. On the other side of the opening, between the Castlehill and the sea, there appears to have existed in times gone by a large sand hill. As long as this dune was stable, it would have served to protect rather than threaten, but when its stability had been removed, for whatever reason, Rattray's fate was in a very literal sense sealed. The writer of the Old Statistical Account of the parish, going on the evidence of local folk memory, suggested that around the year 1720 a furious easterly gale had ripped at the dune and deposited huge quantities of its sand into the vulnerable access channel to the bay.[5] Although some gradual and long-term movement of sand might provide a more realistic picture of what really was happening in the area, the final fate of Rattray may well have been comparatively swift. From the evidence of 19th Century farming improvements on the estate, the laird of Rattray was able to note that sand lay quite distinctly on top of underlying old plough rigs, with no evidence of mixing, suggesting that movement of sand in the past must have been very rapid. Even today, dry spring weather can result in a considerable depth of loose sand on top of exposed soils, and narrow access roads have been rapidly infilled.

According to local tradition the sudden closure of the entrance to Rattray's harbour was indeed so sudden that a small ship loaded with a cargo of roofing tiles or slates was trapped within the harbour, never to set sail into the open sea again. For the farmer at nearby Mains of Haddo, it had been a good illustration of the adage about an ill wind, for he was now able to obtain a ready supply of roofing material for his farm.

As long as its connection with the sea was maintained, Rattray could offer valuable shelter for shipping when easterly gales were blowing. At the end, it was that same easterly wind that was to spell the end for Buchan's remote royal burgh. With its harbour gone, the settlement's demise was assured, and its last residents had to contemplate a new future. A few families continued to gain a living from the sea, having their homes at Seaton, the edge of the village that was closest to the sea, and at a small cluster of settlement known locally as Botany Bay because of its supposed similarity in remoteness to the penal colony in Australia. The severe problems involved in working from the open shore in such an exposed setting meant, however, that most of the remaining families eventually forsook the place in the early 19th Century to seek a fresh start in the new fishing village of Burnhaven near Peterhead. Ironically, this was itself to join the ranks of the lost villages of the north, having been cleared away during the fever of oil-related activity in that corner of Buchan in the 1970's.

*   *   *

If the sealing off of Rattray's outlet to the sea was to be the local people's loss, it was to become the geographer's and naturalist's gain, for it created a fascinating land-locked freshwater loch that is the largest coastal lagoon in Scotland. As the Loch of Strathbeg it has become one of the greatest wetland sites in the north, attracting innumerable ducks, geese and swans to its shallow waters each winter.

Thomas Edward, the famous Banff shoemaker-naturalist of last century was the first to make known the wildlife riches of the place to the outside world.[6] "All the birds of the world come here in winter," the local people told him, and so it must have seemed as the great wildfowl skeins came flighting in to the loch each evening. In recent times, this outstanding wildlife importance was recognised in the designation of the greater part of the Loch of Strathbeg and its margins as a nature reserve by the Royal Society for the Protection of Birds. By means of raised wooden duckboards it is now possible to enter the very heart of the fringing reed beds and see the roosting wildfowl at close range from one of the wooden hides overlooking the water. Greylag and pinkfooted geese occur each year in their thousands, while several hundred Icelandic whooper swans may swell the numbers of home-based mute swans, making up an unforgettable white flotilla on the loch surface. An October visit to the loch can be a most impressive experience as countless excited skeins of geese flight in against the fiery glow of sunset skies, while the whoopers bugle across the water. Added to this may be the rafts of coots and ducks and large flocks of stunningly plumaged wigeon feeding greedily on the grassy bank below the very site of the lost village.

When, in the early 1970's, a plan was unveiled to lay a gas pipeline from the North Sea across the bed of the loch, and to construct a large processing plant nearby, there was a storm of protest. A short time later, however, it was announced that an alternative site had been selected near St Fergus, a few miles further along the Buchan coast. Today, the bright flare of the gas plant can easily be seen from the last ruined remain of the lost village of Rattray. Prosperity was indeed to come to this remote corner, just as the creators of the settlement had hoped, but it was to be from a new resource and long after Rattray's royal burgh had vanished from the face of the land.

1. Milne J (1900) Rattray *Trans Buchan Field Club* Vol V pp 180-207

2. Ibid

3. Hepburn A (1906) Description of Country of Buchan *Macfarlane's Geographical Collections* Vol 1 p40

4. Walton K (1956) Rattray: A Study in Coastal Evolution *Scottish Geographical Magazine* pp 85-96

5. *Old Statistical Account* (1793)

6. Smiles S (1877) *Life of a Scotch Naturalist* p257

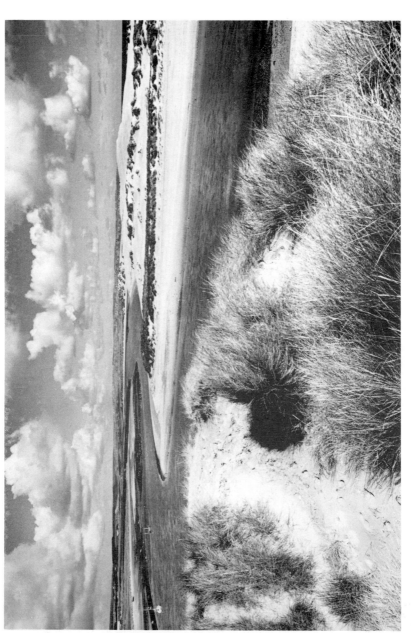

The Ythan estuary and southern tip of the Sands of Forvie from the south.

The middle spine of Forvie from the east where agriculture has bitten into landscape of blown sand.

The heathland and scrub landscape of North Forvie.

The mobile yellow dunes of Forvie in the foreground pass through the middle ground into mature old grey dunes, and eventually the agricultural edge fringing the Ythan estuary.

Old Forvie Kirk.

The signs of prehistoric endeavour in the form of cairns and stone clearance heaps emerge as the dunes migrate in central Forvie.

St Mary's chapel, Rattray.

Sand blow from the fields following ploughing accumulates on the track to the beach near Rattray.

The Loch of Strathbeg with St Mary's chapel on the right horizon.

The former exit channel of the Loch of Strathbeg with Rattray Head lighthouse on the distant horizon.

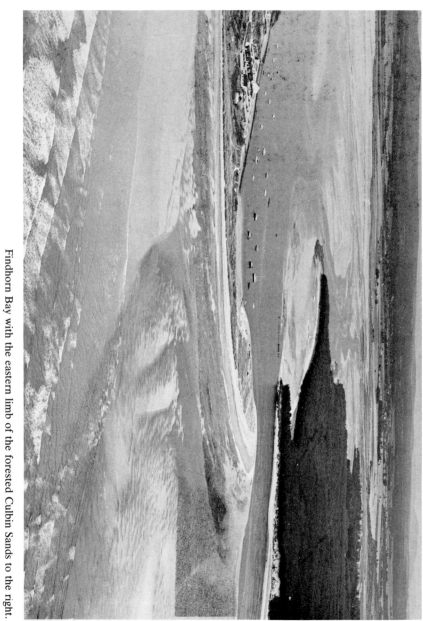

Findhorn Bay with the eastern limb of the forested Culbin Sands to the right.

The forested foreland of Culbin now largely stabilised with the exception of the foredunes along the coastal edge.

The huddled huts of Skara Brae, Skaill, Orkney.

Skara Brae's flagstone furniture of box bed and dresser.

## CULBIN

*Here lay a fair fat land:*
*But now its townships, kirks, graveyards*
*Beneath bald hills of sand*
*Lie buried deep as Babylonian shards.*

Andrew Young
"The Culbin Sands"


Like Forvic, 19th Century Culbin drew visitors to its sandy wastes like a magnet, for this was the age of an all-embracing natural history that found such places utterly irresistable. As a consequence, we have enough contemporary description of this Moray Firth wasteland as it then was to leave us in no doubt of the impact it could make on the human mind. George Bain, editor of the local Nairn Telegraph, wrote: "A scene of greater desolation and dreariness it would be impossible to conceive. For four long miles, and occupying a space of two miles broad, you have nothing but a great sea of sand, rising as it were, in tumultuous billows. The spirit of the scene is its unspeakable loneliness - its utter desolation. As we enter it we observe that the range of sand-hills at the rear end and along the inland margin are here and there covered with patches of tough, struggling bent, flanked by occasional clumps of dwarf plantation. But as we proceed we find nothing in the central track, neither bent nor shrub - nothing but a succession of hills - rising sometimes to the height of 100 feet - all of the finest, lightest, most powdery sand - of sand sparkling in its pearly beauty: of sand so light that its surface is mottled into delicate wave lines by the wind. There is no softness - no speck of colour to relieve the eye - nothing but the fierce unbroken glare of white sand. Your shadow is reflected on the sand with startling distinctness, and your companions a few yards away look like dim, weird figures in the remote distance. You can fancy yourself in the heart of some arid desert - no sound is audible; the murmur of waves on the shore no longer falls upon your ear; the call of the seabird does not reach you; the hum of insect life is awanting; and no voice of man nor cry of beast is heard. Silence reigns supreme. The solitude is absolute and unbroken".[1]

It was those desolate, desert-like qualities of the Culbin Sands which drew the visitors, and which imprint themselves so vividly on the mind today when reading the old accounts. The great 19th Century northern

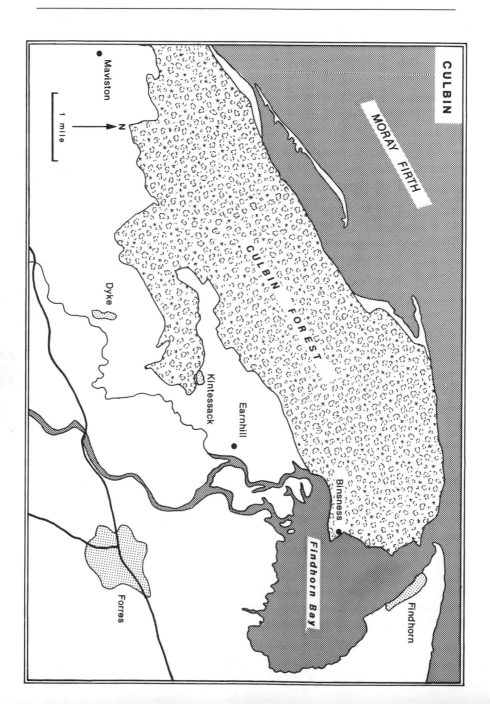

naturalist Charles St John, who was much fascinated by the place, described the finding of human skeletons, supposedly belonging to unfortunate visitors before him who had perished among the sandy wastes.[2]

To appreciate the sheer scale of the Culbin Sands as they then were, it is perhaps sufficient to recall its once common description as "Britain's Desert". On such a broad canvas it was possible for the forces of nature that sifted the sand about to paint a picture of a land of extreme desolation and loneliness. But Culbin on a fine day could be a very different place from Culbin in the teeth of a gale, though few visitors were wont to sample its peculiar attractions in such adverse conditions. An exception was John Martin of Elgin who has left us a vivid account of his experience. "The wind comes rushing down through the openings between the hills, carrying with it immense torrents of sand, with a force and violence almost overpowering. Clouds of dust are raised from the tops of the mounds, and are whirled about in the wildest confusion, and fall with the force of hail. Nothing can be seen but sand above and sand below and sand everywhere. You dare not open your eyes, but must grope your way about as if blindfolded".[3]

The whole impression of the place handed down by those writers who had first-hand knowledge of it is an almost Sahara-like scene, wanting only the characteristic desert accompaniments. But, interestingly enough, this defect was to be unexpectedly remedied towards the end of last century when an irruption of birds took place westwards from the arid wastes of Central Asia. For reasons unknown, vast numbers of Pallas's sand grouse suddenly moved out of their normal breeding area and reached western Europe. Inevitably, they found themselves in an environment very different from that which they had left and many of them soon disappeared. In addition, they had to run the gauntlet of countless bird shooters, for this was the age before enlightened birdwatching, when the philosophy behind bird identification was "what's shot is history, and what's missed is mystery". Such was the similarity between the Culbin Sands and the dry areas from which they had come, however, that unlike the situation in other parts of Britain numbers of Pallas's sand grouse actually stayed on among the Culbin sand hills and nested in the years 1888 and 1889.[4] Predictably, however, ruthless persecution dealt a death blow to these rare visitors from the arid lands of the east, and there is little reminder left of them now, apart from a few fading specimens of the taxidermist's art inside Victorian glass cases.

\* \* \*

As such a desert-like sandy wasteland, Culbin would have seemed a strange contradiction indeed to the folk who knew it in an earlier age. Although distance has a tendency to lend enchantment to the human mind, and doubtless might tend to exaggerate the qualities of an area dramatically removed from farming use, there is enough evidence to suggest that the area's reputation as the meal girnel of Moray would not have been entirely undeserved. The lands of Culbin are mentioned as far back as the 12th Century, and estate rentals suggest the existence of a productive farming landscape right up to the late 17th Century.

In terms of earliest human history, it would appear that there are some parallels with the Forvie situation. The archaeological record suggests that the roots of Culbin's human history go deep in time. Finds of worked flints imply an ancient human presence, but in this particular situation the raw material may have derived from nodules dredged up from the North Sea by the passage of ice during glacial times. The finding of many flint arrow heads is evidence enough for those early folk of Culbin, but the shell middens located in days past must be treated with the same caution as those at the Ythan mouth.

Culbin's location near the mouth of the River Findhorn may go far towards explaining both the productivity of its vanished farmlands and the reason for their disappearance. The lower river valley derived the benefit of countless centuries' deposition of silts, and this, coupled with the climatic advantages of a lowland area in the lee of the hill lands to the south and west, would help to explain the area's reputation for agricultural productivity. The estate rental of the Barony of Culbin for 1693, for example, was £2720 Scots, 640 bolls of bere (a primitive form of barley once widely grown in the north), 640 bolls of wheat, 640 bolls of oats and 640 bolls of oatmeal. These rents paid in kind were typical of estate rents of the time, in which tenants were obliged to supply the fruits of their labours directly in the form of grain or meal from the mill which could then be shipped out or otherwise disposed of by the laird to achieve a cash income. In addition, Culbin's wealth was also based on the productive salmon fishings of the river mouth, exploiting one of the area's most valuable natural resources, the fish which seek the gravel beds of the upper headwaters to spawn. But, equally, the seashore beyond the river mouth was covered in countless tons of fine sand, the product of erosion of the upland interior, especially in times of glacial ice melt.

The 1693 rental of the Culbin lands is therefore of the greatest significance, for it both confirms the productivity of the estate and exists as a finale to it. After this date the resource base of the Culbin area was, in very literal way, to be eroded away by forces of nature as unstoppable as those that had earlier obliterated the village of Forvie and sealed the fate of Rattray's royal burgh.

At the time of the environmental catastrophe which reputedly removed its wealth in one disastrous storm, the Barony of Culbin was in the ownership of the Kinnaird family, represented by its then laird, Alexander. The valuable lands of Culbin in the fertile, low-lying Laigh of Moray had passed into the possession of the Kinnairds during the 15th Century, through a marriage link with the de Moravia family. The Laigh lands consist of a long tract of lowland which gradually emerged from under the sea as the Ice Age waned and the land mass of northern Scotland slowly recovered from its heavy burden of ice. In time, these low-lying lands in the lee of the Monadhliath Mountains were transformed by the labours of generations of farming folk into the fertile tract of farmland that is the Laigh of Moray today.

The Barony of Culbin occupied the area to the west of the Findhorn mouth and, like the rest of the Laigh, enjoyed a reputation for agricultural productivity that would have kept the laird and his family in some comfort and style. Certainly, the mansion house of the Kinnairds was, from all accounts, a building of stature. It possessed its own doocot - a certain pointer to the status of the estate, since Scots law limited the keeping of pigeons for winter meat to those landowners whose estates produced a substantial yearly grain crop. The Culbin doos would certainly not have lacked for food as they foraged over the surrounding farmland, for the Barony possessed its own large home farm and fifteen other smaller ones, as well as numerous small crofts, some of them depending in part or entirely on the local coastal and river fishings.[6] With a land area of about three and a half thousand acres, the Barony of Culbin was clearly an estate of some wealth, and even possessed its own place of worship.

The events leading up to the dramatic effacement of all this from the human landscape of Moray have been colourfully recorded in the writings of various authors, for the history of the place has always been a subject of intense local interest. The climax of the whole developing scenario appears to have been in the year 1694. By the latter part of that year the scene had been set for the greatest environmental change the Moray coastlands had seen since the passing of the great Ice Age. Fierce winds from the west moved great quantities of loose sand eastwards, slowed down only temporarily by the flanking woods of Maviston. George Bain dramatically continues a story with an almost biblical flavour to it: "And it came suddenly and with short warning. A man ploughing had to desert his plough in the middle of the furrow. The reapers in a field of late barley had to leave without finishing their work. In a few hours the plough and the barley were buried beneath the sand. The drift, like a mighty river, came on steadily and ruthlessly, grasping field after field, and enshrouding every object in a mantle of sand. Everything that obstructed its progress speedily became the nucleus of a sand-mound. The old "bins" of sand, uncovered by the uprooting of bent and juniper for thatching purposes, were operated upon, and their contents thrown into the general drift. In terrible gusts the wind carried the sand among the dwelling-houses of the people, sparing neither the hut of the cottar nor the mansion of the laird. The splendid orchard, the beautiful lawn, all shared the same fate. In the morning after the first night of drift, the people had to break through the back of their houses to get out. They relieved the cattle, and drove them to a place of safety. A lull in the storm succeeded, and they began to think they might still have their dwelling-houses, though their lands were ruined for ever. But the storm began again with renewed violence, and they had to flee for their lives, taking with them only such things as they could carry. What a strange scene it must have been - these poor people rushing from their hearths and homes amidst the blinding and bewildering sandstorm. And to add to the horrors of the scene, the sand had choked the mouth of the river Findhorn, which now poured its flooded waters amongst the fields and homesteads, accumulating in lakes and pools till it rose to a height by which it was able to burst the barrier to the north, and find a new outlet to the sea, in its course sweeping to destruction the old village of Findhorn. On returning, the people of Culbin were spellbound. Not a vestige, not a trace of their houses was to be seen. Everything has disappeared beneath the sand".[7]

In his novel "The Fortune of the Sands", James Lorimer paints an imagined picture as seen through the unbelieving eyes of Culbin's laird: "The day before yesterday broke after a night of wild storm such as visits us between Lammas and Martinmas. With the anxiety of one who has become laird barely two years before, I got up and went out at the first streak of light to see whether the offices had suffered any damage. At first I could not but think my eyes were playing a trick on me. The green expanse of the estate on the landward side had turned into a silvery-grey. But, in truth, I could not see much beyond the outskirts of the policies, for a dense cloud of fine sand was driving past my face. When I looked downwards, as perforce I had to, lest I should be blinded, it was to see a thick carpet of sand lying on the lawn. There burst through the hedge of the garden one of my tenants whose farm lay under Mavieston. Ordinarily a douce man and spare of words, he cried in a piteous voice - "For God's sake, Laird, gaither the men at the mains an' come tae oor help or oor ferm-toon'll be smoored i' the sand. It'a broken loose from the hills o'Maviestoon and is comin' doon upo' us like a deluge. The cattle-coorts are buried a'ready an' the san' is up tae the tap o' the windae ahint the hoose".[8]

* * *

A place that had known generations of human toil was now rendered quite useless for human habitation; in short, a desert had been formed. Culbin's laird now found himself transformed from a man of means to a debtor, petitioning Parliament for exemption from the payment of cess or land tax due to the fact that the best part of his estate of Culbin, "by an unavoidable fatality" was quite ruined and destroyed, the direct result of "the overblowing of great and vast heaps of sand, so that there is not a vestige to be seen of my manor place of Culbin, yards, orchards and mains thereof, and which within these twenty years were as considerable as any within the County of Moray".[9]

Alexander Kinnaird's appeal was successful, but his personal future was bleak, for his once productive Barony lands had been largely transformed into a sterile sandy waste. In 1695, the year following the disaster and clearly influenced by it, Parliament took the step of passing an act forbidding the pulling of bent, juniper and broom on sandhills. But, important though the new act was for the future safeguarding of such vulnerable coastal areas elsewhere, it was of little comfort to Culbin's ruined laird. By 1697 he was making an appeal once again to Parliament, this time for personal protection from his creditors. In the summer of the following year the lands of Culbin - for what they were now worth - were sold to Alexander Duff of Drummuir, and a few months later Alexander Kinnaird, devastated by disaster, was dead.

Out of the original sixteen Culbin farms only Earnhill remained. Now the winds that had overblown the estate with sand were allowed free rein to mould and shape the great dunes that reached a hundred feet in places, and which came in time to have their own distinguishing names as landscape features. One of these, Lady Culbin, a gently rounded dune at· the eastern end of the Sands, had the distinction in local folklore of being the sand hill that covered the old mansion house of the Kinnaird lairds.

Indeed, against the background of ignorance of the factors that operate on such an environment, it is hardly surprising that over the years local folk would have created their own pictures of those dramatic events. In particular, the dramatic decline in the fortunes of Alexander Kinnaird demanded some explanation by superstitious minds in terms of the working out of human fate.

Here there appear to be certain strands in the story that would seem to link it with the way in which local folk were wont to interpret the similar Forvie disaster. These appear to have their origins in a desire to attribute such a catastrophic chain of events to some breach against accepted codes of fair dealing and morality. In Forvie's case it was a retribution for an evil act against the helpless and dispossessed rightful owner. The Culbin disaster was attributed to the laird's over-haste to have some local old crones condemned for witchcraft. The predictable curse that followed was considered to have been fulfilled in the engulfing of the Barony by the unprecedented severity of the sand storms.

A second, and even more colourful, interpretation of events is seen in the story of the fateful encounter of Culbin's laird with the Devil. In its way, it is, literally, the familiar theme of the wicked Baron in his castle, or in this case his mansion house, and his involvement in a suitably wicked act, namely a total disregard for the important observance of the Sabbath day. While playing a game of cards on the eve of the Sabbath the laird was reminded that the midnight hour was near, and that engaging in such a practice was an offence against Sabbath observance. Being a strong and independently minded character, however, he was certainly not going to be dictated to by anybody, and asserted that he would go on playing even if the Devil himself were to partner him in the game. Such a reckless statement was clearly tempting fate, however, for, in a mighty clap of thunder the Devil himself suddenly put in an appearance and a long card game was played through, so long, in fact, that the laird failed entirely to notice the drifting sands piling up outside his fine mansion house of Culbin.

\* \* \*

Many and wonderful were such tales told around the winter firesides in the Laigh of Moray in the aftermath of the Culbin disaster. Long after the estate had been swamped by sand, strong winds are said to have brought to the light of day some of the Barony's buried remains. The laird's doocot and Culbin's long-lost place of worship revealed themselves again, initially as objects of awe and wonder and then, in more material terms, as a useful supply of building stone for neighbouring farms. The reappearance of part of the laird's mansion house in all its ghostly grandeur was, inevitably, a source of more than passing local interest. One daring individual is even said to have shouted down a chimney and received back such an eerie echoing reply that it made him take to his heels and run for fear of what else he might encounter! No doubt the inevitable changes in distribution of the sand may have uncovered evidence of the estate's former glory, but it is hard to believe the strongly held local tradition that the laird's long buried orchard trees were able to blossom once more and even to bear fruit. Predictably, the miraculous fruits are invariably remembered as having been of an especially good quality. And the tradition of buried treasure in the form of hidden contraband was also part of local folklore. The precise circumstances are the not unique ones of a valuable cargo of illicit imports being hidden away among the sandhills by smugglers who were later unable to relocate them because of sand movements.[10]

*     *     *

It all seems very familiar, somehow, when set against the story of the Sands of Forvie, but, as at that more southerly location, environmental fact does not accord with the belief in a sudden swamping by sand, Professor Steers, in his classic paper on the area to the Royal Geographical Society half a century ago suggested that the 1695 Act of Parliament anent the pulling of bent suggested that "the destruction was not sudden, but had been extending eastwards for some time. The severe storms of 1694-95 completed the destruction".[11] In other words, they had only dealt the final *coup de grace* to the Barony lands after a long period of environmental deterioration.

Indeed, at the conclusion of Steers' paper, Major R A Bagnold, speaking from considerable experience of sand movement, dismissed the idea of a catastrophic covering of the farms and farmlands. He referred to a calculation which he had made suggesting that "if a wind were to blow over this area for twenty-four hours at an average speed of 40 miles an hour and the sand which the wind carried on to the area were deposited over a depth downward of 1 mile, then the greatest thickness of sand which could be deposited would be only one inch".

Yet, whatever the true time-scale of the sandstorms that finally obliterated the Barony of Culbin, the whole process had dramatically demonstrated the vulnerability of some of the adjoining farmlands to further inundation by sand. It is not surprising, therefore, that several of the local landowners had established early schemes of tree planting on the fringes of the Culbin sandhills. Grant of Kincorth was prominent in early 19th century pioneer planting, establishing a tree cover on Culbin's eastern flank, and this was followed by the work of others who managed successfully to plant the more stable sands in what came to be known as the Low Wood. Later in the century Chadwick of Binsness was busy planting Corsican pines on the sandy lands of his estate directly across the bay from the present day Findhorn village. In recent times some of this early Binsness planting has been able to serve as a measure of the extent of change that can occur through sand movement, with fairly tall trees being buried almost to their tops among sand drifts.

But if these pioneer estate owners laid the foundations of the transformation of Culbin from desert wasteland to productive plantation, it was the Forestry Commission that was to carry the work through to the establishment of a flourishing forest[12]. Commencing in 1921, the Commission began the long task of acquiring land at Culbin. Such a vast scheme of tree planting in an environment so unstable as the sandhills clearly called for an original approach that was inevitably characterised by trial and error. Even within today's maturing plantations, incongruous-looking clumps of maritime marram grass may be seen. These relics of a more open landscape are pointers to the early attempts to arrest sand movement by establishing the deep-rooting marram into the sand. In this way it was possible to protect the young transplant trees to some extent from shifting sand which might either expose their roots to dessication or suffocate them completely.

In time, the technique of thatching the mobile dunes was adopted and found to be most successful. Established woodlands from miles around were cleared of their conifer brushwood and "weedings" of birch and broom. The weight of branches laid closely together was sufficient to hold the thatch in place, even in times of strong wind, and pegging down was even successful on the highest and most exposed dunes, as in the case of Hill 99. With a summit height of ninety-nine feet this was one of the highest dunes, and it was successfully planted with Corsican pine in 1937 and 1938, following some of the earliest thatching operations. In a short time the seedling trees which had been planted into the protective cover of thatching material could derive the benefit of a good ground mulch round about them, as well as the organic feeding from break down of the leaf matter. Once established, the plantations themselves were capable of providing their own moisture-retaining mulch in the thick layer of pine needles above the sandy forest floor. The general planting strategy employed over the whole area was to move gradually across the sands from west to east, thus affording more and more protection as time went on for the newest plantations, since the major wind influence is a westerly one.

The pioneering work of tree planting on the Binsness estate had already demonstrated the suitability of the exotic Corsican pine for the work of dune afforestation. Although considerably to the north of its south European homeland, this species is well adapted to withstanding the extremely dry environment of a sand dune system. In addition, with its Mediterranean island background, it is suited to withstanding the sea breezes off the Moray Firth. Unexpectedly, perhaps, the Corsican pine was found to have a more favourable growth rate than the native Scots pine, although this is the other most widely planted species.

The North American lodgepole pine, so named from the practice of Red Indians using its long, straight poles as supports for the skin walls of their lodges, has been planted to a more limited extent in areas like the former winter lochs which provided a particular challenge. Maritime pine and Monterey pine are also established on a smaller scale still, but are environmentally much less suited to the rigorous conditions at Culbin.

The strategic needs of wartime resulted in the felling of great tracts of the early plantings established by the far-seeing estate owners of the past, and some of the surviving old trees fell victim to the great gale of January, 1953 which so devastated the forests of North-east Scotland. But such losses have been more than compensated for by the massive scheme of dune afforestation carried through by the Forestry Commission in the course of this century. The establishment of duneland forest has been accomplished elsewhere around the British coast, as at Holkham Meals in Norfolk and at Newborough Warren on the island of Anglesey. At Newborough, interestingly enough, in a direct parallel to the Culbin situation, a large area of arable land was engulfed by moving sand in mediaeval times.[13] And the comparison is even more interesting when it is learned that the disaster there was attributed to the habit of local folk of pulling the marram, though in this particular case it was for basket weaving. Culbin's achievement, however, remains unique. In its massive tree planting schemes "Britain's Desert" has been transformed into Britain's greatest coastal forest, and the lost Barony of Culbin now lies beneath a covering mantle of pines.

\* \* \*

In their transformation from economically worthless desert to productive state forest, the Culbin Sands underwent the most dramatic landscape personality change. As a result, the ecological interest of the area was radically transformed. Pallas's sand grouse would certainly find nothing to attract it to the area today. Even the indigenous red grouse which once haunted the heathery edges has long since vanished, but in its place has come a more spectacular game bird by far, the woodland-dwelling capercaillie. Once eradicated from its native pinewood habitat of the north, the capercaillie was reintroduced to the Highlands last century and now finds an ecological niche among the pine stands of Culbin.

Indeed, there is more than a passing resemblance between the oldest Culbin plantations and the native forests of Speyside which represent some of the last fragments of the ancient Caledonian pinewoods. The crusty-barked mature pines with their green understorey closely resemble the conditions within the old forest, and it is therefore no surprise to find a representative selection of the characteristic plant and wildlife association. In addition to the capercaillie, red squirrel, great spotted woodpecker, crested tit and crossbill are all found in the Culbin plantations, and even ospreys may occasionally be seen fishing in the adjacent shallows of Findhorn Bay. Crested tits were once confined to the Speyside pinewoods which fulfilled their breeding requirements, but now the old Culbin plantings have given them a coastal extension to their valley habitat, and a valuable addition to their hitherto highly restricted range. Butterflies also find the open character of some of the planted areas an attraction, perhaps the most interesting being the Scots argus which may be seen sunning itself along open rides during bright summer days.

For an essentially man-created forest environment, Culbin is remarkably well endowed in unusual plant species. The greenish-brown coral-root is a strange orchid that finds its desired growing conditions among the tree roots. The uncommon wintergreens have drawn botanists to seek out their representative species, but it is not only such lovely flowers of the summer pinewoods that make Culbin Forest one of the most significant northern ecological sites. Autumn days bring their own rewards, and a fungal foray among the tree roots and needle-strewn forest floor reveals an extraordinary variety of toadstools and mushrooms.

The botanical richness of the place is clearly considerable, but for Steers, the geographer, writing in the 1930s when afforestation was nowhere near complete, there were regrets over the extraordinary character change, when he wrote: "Whilst the afforestation has once again made Culbin a valuable national asset .... the physiographer cannot help regretting that the nearest approach to a desert in the British Isles is rapidly disappearing".[14] And now, half a century on, "Britain's Desert" is just a memory, though fortunately preserved in photographs and in the evocative descriptions of writers like George Bain.

The geographer's loss has indeed become the forester's gain, but perhaps as the wind soughs among the Culbin pines it may stir the ghost of a ruined laird whose lands now lie deep beneath the drifting sands.

1. Bain G (nd) *The Culbin Sands* p12

2. Ibid p14

3. Ibid p13

4. Baxter E V & Rintoul L J *The Birds of Scotland* p530

5. MacGregor A A (1949) *The Buried Barony* p4

6. Bain G p16

7. Ibid p19

8. Lorimer J (1934) *The Fortune of the Sands. A Romance of Moray* p1

9. Macgregor A A p5

10. Shaw L (1882) *A History of the Province of Moray* p221

11. Steers J A (1937) The Culbin Sands and Burghead Bay *Geographical Journal* Vol 90 pp 498-523

12. Forestry Commission (1949) *Britain's Forests. Culbin* p2

13. Eyre S R (1968) *Vegetation and Soils. A World Picture* p192

14. Steers J A *op cit*

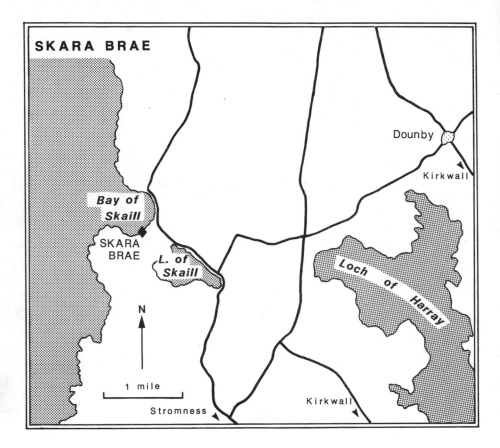

## SKARA BRAE

*The Weem of Scara Brae, one of the most remarkable series of primitive dwellings known*

J R Tudor, 1883

Although the so-called "Stone-Age" village of Skara Brae is yearly gazed upon by hundreds of visitors to Orkney, its very existence was a complete unknown to the generations of Orcadians who lived and farmed beside it in that western fringe of their main island. But all this was to be quite dramatically changed in 1850 when a storm of exceptional severity, even by Orkney standards, lashed the land and tore at the vegetation cover binding together a sandhill overlooking the Bay of Skaill. This resulted in the blowing of great quantities of sand from the dune, locally known as Skerrabrae. What was then uncovered, to the great interest of the local laird was the edge of a strange underlying mound of hard-packed material and the remains of ancient human habitation. This extraordinary assemblage of long-lost village remains embedded in an ancient midden heap was, indeed, to become one of the most significant archaeological sites ever, for Skara Brae is recognised as the best preserved prehistoric village in the whole of northern Europe.

Following the remarkable uncovering of the edge of the settlement, in the next few years William Watt, laird of Skaill, set about further excavation of the revealed remains. By 1924 the site had been entrusted into the care of HM Commissioner of Works, which was perhaps just as well since a further severe storm was soon to tear away part of the coast and also the midden heap and the previously excavated remains. A sea wall was quickly erected to prevent further marine erosion, and in 1927 proper examination commenced. The following year Professor Gordon Childe was invited to go north to supervise this important work. For Childe this was to be an exciting challenge that was to stretch his imagination over many months of patient excavation and recording. "When I reached the site that year, Skara Brae appeared as a grass-grown sand-dune from the seaward edge of which protruded the ruinous walls of five huts and some sections of a connecting passageway".[1] Without any doubt this was destined to be the most sensational reappearance ever of a sand-swamped lost village.

\* \* \*

Until his excavation of the buried remains of Skara Brae, the recon-

49

struction of everyday scenes of prehistoric domestic life had been, as Childe himself observed, "a work of pure imagination". Skara Brae was to rectify all this, however. As Childe observed, "Here a gigantic sand dune has embalmed a whole complex of huts and lanes, preserving even their walls to a height of eight or nine feet; lack of timber had obliged their builders to translate into stone, and thus perpetuate articles of furniture usually constructed of perishable wood".[2]

Nearly half a century later, further excavation had the benefit of modern advanced dating techniques not available to Childe.[3] As a result, the occupation of Skara Brae has been revealed by radio carbon dating to have begun around 3100 BC and to have lasted approximately six hundred years. What the modern visitor to the Bay of Skaill is drawn, therefore, to see is a village cluster of huts thousands of years old, each one stone-built to a roughly rectangular plan. Careful excavation and continuity of care have together ensured the continued survival of the huts and their interior plenishings, so that the unpractised eye and mind need not struggle too hard to imagine what things may have been like in those distant island days.

What ensured the survival of this ancient lost village, apart from its burial by sand, was the fact of its translation into stone, as Childe put it. Skaill's early dwellers were surrounded by the abundant wealth of a natural resource - the varied local types of the Old Red Sandstone that had been deposited millions of years before in the vast Lake Orcadie. Even today the coastal edge reveals the wealth of flagstones whose bedding planes have split into a varied assortment of once useful slabs. Also outcropping locally is a very fine-grained sedimentary rock resembling slate, and useful throughout Orcadian history for roofing purposes. With such an abundance of versatile building stone so close at hand, the Skara Brae folk were not too incommoded by the absence of suitable growing timber. Indeed, this ubiquitous use of stone as a construction medium for walls and fitments has been the means of preserving a unique window on Orkney's most ancient human past.

During excavation it became clear that the site first revealed in 1850 had actually been built into an existing midden remain, clearly indicating a continuity of settlement on the site. Only the very tops of the underground houses would have protruded above the encircling midden, so that the largely subterranean Neolithic village would have derived the benefit of shelter from the wind. The villagers of Skara Brae must, therefore, have enjoyed a cosy if dark existence in their interconnecting dwellings. Clearly, the surrounding presence of domestic refuse must also go far towards accounting for the site's unusual state of preservation.

*   *   *

The hut walls are low and slightly corbelled inwards, that is to say there is a gradual inward projection starting from the base. No further dressing of the flagstone building material was necessary to make it highly suitable for drystone construction, and for the provision of ambries or keeping places for personal possessions in the structure of the walls. This wall-recess tradition was a long continued one in Orkney, and even in today's human landscape the inner walls of ruined croft houses often reveal features that are the product of an ancient stone-building tradition.

As in so many early rural house building traditions the hearth was the heart of the individual Skara Brae dwelling, the central focus of family life, and situated in the middle of the floor. Less predictable are the open boxes made from very thin stone slabs set into the floor and apparently joined at the seams with clay. These are generally considered to have been water holding tanks in which limpets were stored, possibly more as fishing bait than as human food.

Perhaps the crowning glory of the Skara Brae huts to the first-time visitor must be the stone-built structures we may call dressers, the Neolithic forerunners to today's unit furniture. And yet, almost as remarkable in their appearance, and arguably more interesting, are the stone beds formed from large flagstones built out from the wall on either side of the hearth. Two slabs set on edge protrude out of the wall and a third is laid lengthwise to join them, forming a rectangular-shaped sleeping compartment that would have been lined with locally gathered vegetation. Such an arrangement has also clearly been a long continued northern tradition, for almost identical arrangements made of wood could still be found in old Norwegian peasant houses early this century.

The fronts of the Skara Brae beds are flanked on either side by flagstone pillars, the purpose of which may well be made clear by reference to Dr Arthur Mitchell's description of a Hebridean box bed at the end of the last century. "They [the beds] usually consist simply of four rough, upright posts bound together by narrow side stretchers, on which rests a wooden bottom covered with loose straw. The two uprights which are farthest from the wall often reach the rafters, and are attached to them by straw ropes. Upon these there is a sort of inner roof constructed and this inner roof is often covered with divots. The need of this roof-within-a-roof depends on the fact that the outer roof is often far from water-tight. All ages and sexes occupy these beds".[4]

* * *

The subsistence living of the Skara Brae folk must have been strongly sustained by pastoral farming, to judge by the abundance of cattle and sheep bones in the midden. Indeed, the farming landscape of the coastal fringe at Skaill in those far off times may not have been dissimilar to that at Forvie. The seashore would also have strongly complemented the machair strip as a resource base for these early Orcadians, and indeed was to do so for their successors throughout many ensuing centuries.[5] Fish bones and shells testify to the fact that this littoral resource was exploited to the full. The natural resources of the island interior were not neglected either, as finds such as hazel nut shells and deer bones would indicate.

And then there was the tide's occasional largesse. Today's beachcombers maintain a long island tradition, and although the precise configuration of the coast at Skaill may have been slightly different in the past, it seems likely that driftwood would have been as assiduously sought by the Skara Brae folk as it is to this day in the treeless islands. Even lumps of pumice rock, their air-filled interstices keeping them buoyant in the water, must have landed upon the shore, presumably drifted down from the volcanic north. Its abrasive properties would have been as much appreciated by the Skara Brae folk as they are today, though a modern Orcadian is more likely to obtain his pumice block from the chemist's shop than from the shore.

All in all, the picture which painstaking archaeological excavation has revealed of Skara Brae is of an almost totally concealed village cluster, set deep within the ancient midden heap of an even earlier settlement, whose inhabitants pursued a life of self-sufficiency. Supported by the natural resources of the island scene, their lives were lived in a style strikingly evoked by the legacy of material remains which lay hidden for so long beneath their covering blanket of blown sand.

Precisely why the settlement may have been abandoned is still a matter of conjecture among prehistorians, though Professor Childe was in less doubt, postulating some sudden dramatic abandoning of the settlement as sand swept across it. Once again, however, the known speed of movement of blowing sand would not support the suggestion of a totally unexpected, catastrophic swamping of the site.

Whatever the exact circumstances of its disappearance from the visible cultural landscape of Mainland Orkney, the dramatic reappearance of the lost village of Skara Brae has provided us with a fascinating window on the day-to-day life of the island's most ancient past. The domestic scene of the folk, so lastingly expressed in their use of the local stone, is uniquely presented to the island visitor today in this sand-buried Neolithic time capsule. But in Orcadian terms the site must also be valued for what it reveals about the continuity of human tradition in that northern setting. Drystone walls with recessed keeping places and beds that were part of the fitments of the house were as familiar to 18th and even 19th Century country folk in Orkney as they were to their ancient forebears at the Bay of Skaill. Past and present, expressed in the homely traditions of ordinary folk, would seem to come very close together in this northern island setting.

Perhaps it might be said that the ancient lost village of Skara Brae with all its rich remains relieves the imagination of too much effort in trying to picture the ancient domestic past. But material remains are only an expression of material culture; they say nothing of the thoughts and feelings of the people who left them. It would be nice to imagine that after a winter spent in the dank gloom of that great midden heap, the inhabitants of this most celebrated of sand-swamped villages cheered to the sight of the lovely blue-flowered oyster plant that still opens to the summer sun along the Bay of Skaill.

1. Childe, V G (1931) *Skara Brae. A Pictish Village in Orkney* p5

2. Ibid p1

3. Childe V G & Clarke D V (1983) *Skara Brae* p6

4. Mitchell A (1880) *The Past in the Present* p52

5. Willis, D P (1983) *Moorland and Shore. Their Place in the Human Geography of Old Orkney* O'Dell Memorial Monograph No 14 University of Aberdeen Department of Geography p14